Tyler Does Not Have Contact With His Dad in Prison

Lorna Brookes and
Emily Livsey

Illustrated by Aoife J O'Dwyer

≫ WATERSIDE PRESS

From the My Parent in Prison Series

Tyler's Dad is in prison.

Tyler lives with Mum, his older
brother Ben and their dog Buddy.

Tyler misses Dad. He has not seen
him since Dad went to prison.

Tyler is drawing at the table while
Mum works on her laptop. He asks
Mum *"When can I visit Dad in prison?"*

Mum feels sad. She has to talk to
Tyler about something difficult.

Mum is worried. She knows Tyler cannot visit
Dad in prison. This would not be safe for Tyler.

She knows Tyler misses Dad
and loves him very much.

She does not know how to tell Tyler he
cannot have any contact with Dad.

Tyler's and Ben's social worker comes to visit.
He helps Mum to explain to Tyler and Ben
why they cannot have contact with Dad.

"It's not fair" Tyler says. *"Other
children go on prison visits!"*

Tyler runs out of the room crying.

The social worker comforts Tyler.
Tyler is drawing pictures because
this helps him to calm down.

"I know this is very hard" says the social worker.

*"But the most important thing is that
you, Mum and Ben are safe".*

Ben and Tyler take Buddy for a walk.

Tyler is very quiet. He is still sad about Dad.

Ben says *"I know this feels rubbish, but it is for the best. We didn't always feel safe before and that was very hard"*.

The next time the social worker comes to visit, Tyler is drawing a picture of Buddy.

Tyler says *"I wish I could give Dad my picture"*. Ben says *"I wish Dad knew how we felt".*

The social worker explains that if Tyler wants to draw pictures, and Ben wants to write down his feelings this might help. *"Perhaps you can keep what you write and draw, and things that remind you of Dad, in a special box?"*

Dear Dad,
DAD
DAD
LOVE,
TYLER

Tyler, Ben, Mum and Buddy are at the park.

Tyler sees a poster for a funfair with rides.

"We can go next week" says Mum.

"I can't wait" says Tyler. *"I'm sad I can't tell Dad about the funfair but I know this is for the best".*

Tyler feels excited about the fair.

17

That evening Tyler gets out his art
set. He knows that art helps him
to feel happy and relaxed.

Tyler shows his new drawing to Mum. "That's
amazing", says Mum and she puts what
he has drawn up on the kitchen wall.

Tyler feels proud.

We are a service that supports children and young people who have a parent or family member in prison. We also support children and young people before a parent has gone to prison if it is likely they will go into custody, and after a parent has been released.

We were established in 2017 under the name 'MyTime' before changing our name to Time-Matters. We also provide training for organizations who wish to set up a similar service in their own geographical area.

Where are we?

We are based in Merseyside in the UK, but we welcome children from any locality. We are not affiliated to any particular prison; rather our support is community-based. Support takes place face-to-face in various venues including community centres, youth clubs, schools, and online.

What do we do?

Peer Support Groups: Therapeutic support groups enable children and young people to discuss their feelings and consider coping strategies with trained practitioners and other young people who share their experience. Normally there are around 5–15 children in a group. Groups might be face-to-face or online. We address difficult issues, but we also have fun. We are child and youth centred. We believe our groups help build resilience in children and young people.

1:1 Mentoring: Children and young people are able to access bespoke 1:1 mentoring delivered by trained volunteers. We know that every child is different and every experience of having a parent or family member in prison is different. These sessions are therefore really helpful for children to explore their feelings, in a more private setting, with one mentor who takes the time to get to know their personality, interests and particular challenges they might want help with.

Children as Changemakers: We see the children and young people who attend our service as experts of their own experience. We provide them with the opportunity to be leaders and